P9-DEW-052

1400	1500	1600	1700	1800	1900	2000

1493–1541
Paracelsus
(Philippus Aureolus
Theophrastus Bombastus
von Hohenheim),
Swiss doctor

1543
Vesalius Andreas
(1514–64), Flemish
anatomist and writer,
publishes his discoveries
about human anatomy,
based on the dissection
of bodies

c. 1510–90
Ambrose Paré, French
surgeon, sewed up
wounds instead of
pouring hot oil on them

late 16th century
microscopes invented by
Dutch eyeglass-makers

1628
William Harvey
(1578–1657), English doctor
and anatomist, publishes
his findings on the way
that the heart pumps
blood around the body

1796
Edward Jenner
(1749–1823), English
doctor, first vaccinates
against smallpox

1794–1847
Robert Liston,
Scottish surgeon famed
for speedy amputations

1829
William Burke
(1792–1829), Irish
laborer, hanged in
Edinburgh for
murdering people
and selling their
bodies, on the evidence
of his partner, William
Hare (c.1790–c.1860)

1837–1901
Reign of Queen Victoria

1842
Crawford Long (1815–78),
American doctor, first uses
ether as an anesthetic

1865
— Joseph Lister (1827–1912)
introduces antiseptics
— Queen Victoria uses
chloroform as an
anesthetic

1928
Alexander Fleming
(1881–1955), Scottish
scientist, discovers
penicillin

1957
first small heart
pacemaker invented

1972
— CAT scan introduced
by British engineer
Godfrey Newbold
Hounsfield
— Keyhole surgery
first used

1981
AIDS recognized
as a disease

2000
Scientists announce the
mapping of the human
genome

2002
An American company
announces it may have
an AIDS vaccine by 2005

The story of
Medicine

from acupuncture to X rays

JUDY LINDSAY

OXFORD
UNIVERSITY PRESS

In association with the British Museum Press

With thanks to my Dad, himself a doctor,
who took some of the photos and appears in the last chapter

Published in the United States of America by
Oxford University Press, Inc.
198 Madison Avenue, New York, NY 10016
www.oup.com
Oxford is a registered trademark of Oxford University Press, Inc.

First published in 2003 by The British Museum Press
A division of The British Museum Company Limited
46 Bloomsbury Street, London WC1B 3QQ

ISBN 0-19-521984-8

Library of Congress Cataloging-in-Publication data is available.
Designed and typeset in ITC Golden Cockerall by Peter Burgess, Oxford.
Printed and bound in Hong Kong by Paramount Printing Co.

▶ **What we look like inside.**
A 16th-century drawing of
a human skeleton leaning
on a shovel.

Illustration Acknowledgments

Photographs are taken by the Photography and
Imaging Department of The British Museum and ©
The Trustees of The British Museum unless otherwise
stated.

Ancient Art and Architecture Collection
    15 bottom right, 18 bottom left
Tim Beddow/Science Photo Library
    27 bottom
Susan Bird 9 bottom, 12 bottom
The British Library 6 left, 7 bottom left,
    10 top right, 11 top, 16 bottom, 20 right,
    21 bottom right, 22 bottom right, 25 bottom right, 26
    top left, 28 top right,
    30 top left, 37 bottom left
BSIP VEM/Science Photo Library
    37 bottom right
Dr Jeremy Burgess/Science Photo Library 26 bottom
    and front cover (right)
Peter Burgess, chapter opener drawings
    on pages 6, 10, 14, 18, 20, 24, 28, 32, 36, 38
Joyce Filer 24 bottom right
Griffith Institute 21 top left
Ralph Jackson 22 top left
Kings College Hospital NHS Trust
    31 top right
Lesley and Roy Adkins Picture Library 15 top
Dr Ken Lindsay 5 bottom, 38 bottom left,
    39 top
Mary Evans Picture Library 13 top
National Medical Slide Bank 38 top right

NIBSC/Science Photo Library 31 bottom
Old Operating Theatre 8 bottom.
Richard Parkinson 10 bottom left
The Royal Free Hospital, London front cover (left)
Richard Revels 21 centre
Françoise Sauze/Science Photo Library
    36 bottom right
Science Museum/Science and Society Picture Library
    6 right, 13 bottom left,
    23 top (NMPFT/Science & Society Photo Library),
    23 bottom, 24 top right, 25 centre,
    26 top right, 30 bottom left (Manchester Daily
    Express/Science & Society Photo Library), 39
    bottom right
Dr Linda Stannard, UCT/Science Photo Library 31 top
    left
Maximilian Stock/Science Photo Library
    13 bottom right
Thackray Medical Museum 17 bottom,
    20 bottom left
Tim Vernon, St James University Hospital, Leeds 37 top
    left, 39 bottom left
Wellcome Library, London 3, 5 top, 7 top,
    7 centre, 8 top, 9 top, 11 bottom right,
    12 top, 16 top, 17 top, 19 top right, 22 top right, 24 left,
    27 top left, 27 top right,
    29 top left, 29 bottom right, 30 bottom right, 36
    bottom left
York Archaeological Trust Photographic Unit, photo
    by Derek Phillips 15
    bottom left

Contents

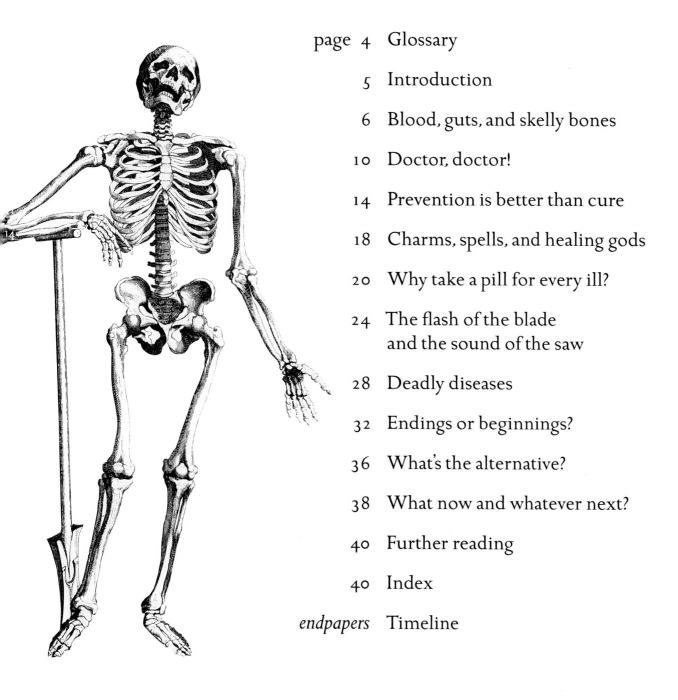

Glossary

abscess a swelling filled with pus

acupuncture an ancient Chinese treatment using small needles, inserted into the body at important 'pressure points' to stimulate the nerves

amulet a magical charm used to ward off illness

anesthetic something that puts a patient to sleep or numbs a part of the body

anatomy the study of what's inside our bodies

antiseptic a substance that destroys the harmful micro-organisms that can cause infection

aqueduct channels built by the Romans to carry water from one place to another, often incorporating bridges and canals

Ayurvedic Medicine classical Indian medical teaching. Ayurveda means "the knowledge needed for long life"

bacteria the group of harmful micro-organisms that cause disease

bile bitter fluid produced by the liver

carbolic acid antiseptic mixture of chemicals discovered by a German chemist in 1830

CAT scan a three-dimensional X ray

cauterize to destroy infected tissue or stop bleeding by burning

chloroform colorless, sweet-tasting liquid that causes unconsciousness if inhaled

diagnosis identifying a disease from its symptoms

dissection the practice of cutting open bodies to see what is inside

epidemic a widespread outbreak of disease that affects many people

ether colourless liquid used as an anaesthetic

excrement waste matter left after food has been digested

exorcise to drive away an evil spirit

genetics the study of our genes, the blueprints that determine the characteristics of plants and animals

Hippocratic Oath an oath, first taken by students of Hippocrates, in which doctors promise they will only use their skills to help patients

kaolin fine, soft white clay used in medicines

massage stroking, pressing, rubbing, or manipulating the body

micro-organism an organism so small it can only be seen using a microscope

organism living plant or animal

palaeopathologist someone who studies prehistoric diseases

pharmacist somebody legally qualified to dispense drugs and medicines

physiology the study of how our bodies work

physician someone legally allowed to be a doctor

prescription written instructions from a doctor on what medicines a patient should take

pustule pimple or lump filled with pus

remedy anything used to cure a disease or illness

salve soothing ointment

shaman a priest who uses magic to heal the sick

surgery treating a patient by cutting, splinting or manipulating the body

symptom bodily signs that help a doctor identify what illness a patient is suffering from

vaccination deliberately infecting a patient with something fairly harmless to make them immune to a specific disease

virus tiny micro-organism that can cause infection

X ray a photograph of the inside of the body

Introduction

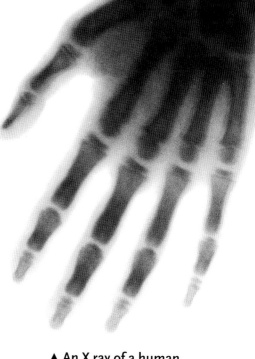

Today you don't need to be a doctor to know a good deal about your body and how it works. We learn all about the heart, lungs, nerves, arteries, and veins in school. We know that we should eat our greens and drink plenty of milk to get the vitamins and minerals that keep our skin, bones, and teeth healthy. You may have taken iron supplements, some cough syrup or an aspirin if you have been feeling a bit under the weather. You probably know what a skeleton looks like, and may even have seen an X ray of some of your own bones.

If you feel sick, you will most likely go and find a useful and reliable adult and tell them what the matter is. If you are snuffly and sneezy and have a sore throat, you will probably be told that you are suffering from a common cold and you should drink fluids and go to bed. If you have cut yourself, then you can be pretty sure that the cut will be washed, then some antiseptic cream and a bandaid will do the trick.

If you are too sick to be looked after at home, the useful and reliable adult will take you to a doctor, who knows even more about bodies and how they work. The doctor will try to find out what is wrong with you and give you something to make you better. If the doctor can't do that, you may be sent to a hospital to have special tests or an operation. In the modern world we have become very good at avoiding getting ill and at treating sickness when we do.

But this wasn't always the case. Every civilization has its own healers and its own way of dealing with people who are unwell, but until recently there was a great deal we didn't know about the human body, and that limited what doctors could do to help. Even today people use many different ways of healing—there is no right way or wrong way of making sick people better. The story of how medicine developed is a fascinating journey through many countries over a long period of time.

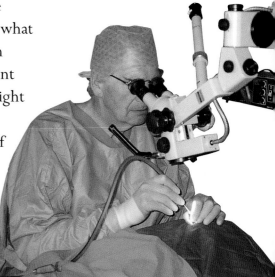

▼ This doctor is examining a patient's ear using an operating microscope.

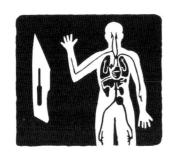

Blood, guts, and skelly bones…
Finding out how the body works

Anatomy is the study of what parts make up our bodies. "Physiology" means finding out how the body works. "Dissection" means cutting a body open to find out more about anatomy and physiology.

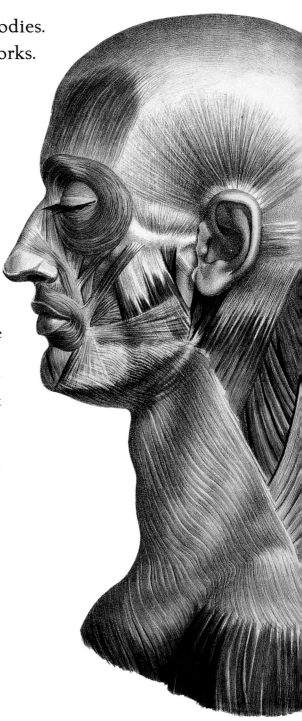

The mysterious body

Thousands of years ago people had never seen inside a human being. In many cultures dissection was forbidden for religious reasons or because people thought it was disrespectful to cut bodies open. In ancient China only the emperor was allowed to dissect bodies. In India, cutting a dead body with a knife was strictly forbidden, so the only way to study the inside of a body was to store it under water until the skin became soft enough to be poked away with a stick.

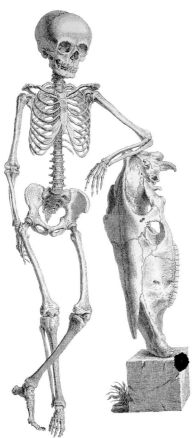

▲ A drawing of a skeleton (and friend) made in 1733.

▶ What lies just under your skin: muscles and blood vessels.

In the classical world, Greek doctors like Hippocrates (c. 460–c. 375 BC) and Galen (AD 129–216), whose books on anatomy were very famous, almost certainly never dissected a human body. Their knowledge of anatomy was based on animals, which are quite different inside from humans. The result was that for a long time doctors had some strange ideas about how the body works.

▲ Galen was a Greek doctor who worked for the Romans. Much of his anatomical knowledge came from dissecting animals.

Things started to change during the Middle Ages, when Italian doctors at the universities of Padua and Bologna took to dissecting human bodies rather than animals in an attempt to correct some of Galen's mistakes. The first public dissection of a human body took place in Bologna in 1315. However, people still did not like the thought of cutting bodies open, and Italian doctors had to use the bodies of convicted criminals!

▼ Doctors in the 13th century knew how to take a pulse, but they did not know how blood was pumped around the body.

Bodies in a bedroom

As times moved on, ideas changed. More dissections took place, and people began to find out a great deal more about anatomy and physiology. Then two important discoveries really changed the way we think about the human body. The first was made by Andreas Vesalius (1514–64), who was born in Brussels in the Low Countries and received his medical degree from Padua in Italy in 1537.

▶ Andreas Vesalius's 1543 book on anatomy included some of the first accurate drawings of the human skeleton and muscles.

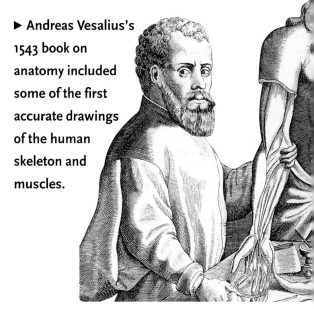

He was determined to find out more about anatomy, and was rumored to have fought wild dogs for bodies in Italian graveyards. He kept these bodies in his bedroom, where he cut them open and studied them in detail. In 1543 Vesalius published a book based on his studies, with hundreds of illustrations of the inside of the body. The book wasn't quite perfect, but it corrected many of Galen's more obvious mistakes.

Digging up the dead

After these discoveries were made people began to realize how important dissection was. However, bodies were still hard to obtain. This led to the rise of a rather gruesome new trade—that of the resurrection men, who went around at night robbing graves so that they could sell the bodies to doctors and medical schools. They roamed around in the dead of night with shovels and body bags. Then, in the early 1800s, two Irishmen went one step further.

Heart to heart

The second important discovery was made a century later by an Englishman, William Harvey (1578-1657). Harvey was a bad-tempered doctor who was obsessed with dissection, and cut open dogs, cats, rats, and even snakes! Earlier doctors had only had vague ideas about how the heart pumped blood around the body. Harvey's experiments proved that blood moves from one side of the heart into the lungs, where it absorbs oxygen, and is then pumped back into the heart. Arteries carry blood away from the heart to all the different parts of the body, and the veins carry it back.

▲ Lock up your pets! William Harvey and later doctors would dissect almost anything to find out more about anatomy.

▼ In Victorian times medical students learned about anatomy by watching dissections in operating theaters like this one.

Medicine and murder

There was a big medical school in Edinburgh, Scotland, so the market for bodies to dissect was huge. So huge, in fact, that William Burke (1792-1829) and William Hare (c.1790-c.1860) found they couldn't meet the demand just by robbing graves. Burke owned a boarding house, and he and his companion took to murdering guests and selling their bodies. They murdered 16 people and made a pretty penny before they were caught in 1829.

Nowadays people aren't so bothered about dissection, and many people actually leave their bodies to medical science to be studied after they die.

▶ **One of Burke and Hare's victims comes to an unpleasant end.**

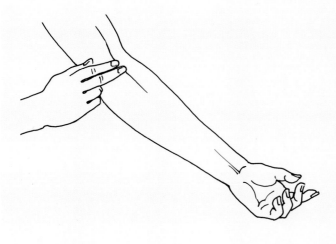

Here is an experiment to do at home. Hold out your right forearm and see if you can find a vein—they look like blue lines lying just under your skin. Now, run your finger along the vein from the crook of your elbow toward your wrist—but don't lift your finger off when you reach the end! You should find that the blueness disappears. That's because the blood empties out of the vein, which stays empty until you remove your finger. Now try it in the other direction, from your wrist to your elbow. You should find that the blood simply refills the vein as your finger moves. What direction do you think the blood is flowing in?

Doctor, doctor!
How did healers learn their trade?

NOWADAYS doctors train for many years before they begin their work. But for as long as people have fallen ill there have been healers who have tried to make them better. Without written records it is hard to know what those healers would have been like in prehistoric times, but looking at societies that have kept their traditional ways of healing can give us some clues. In Australia, Aboriginal medicine men sing to their patients, or violently suck the infected part of the body. This is quite like rituals used by Native American healers, in which shamans call on supernatural powers to heal the sick. These rituals are used alongside simple herbal cures.

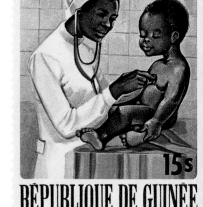

▲ Until quite recently most doctors were men. Now women all over the world train to be doctors.

Father to son

Early civilizations also had doctors, although often they were not really separate from priests and magicians. In ancient Egypt all three worked together, each using a different approach. The priests called upon divine powers to heal the sick, magicians wove spells and incantations against evil spirits, and doctors examined their patients and prescribed remedies. There were no medical schools in ancient Egypt, and most doctors learned their trade from their families. Medical information was written on scrolls made from papyrus reed. These scrolls served as textbooks. They gave advice on how to examine the patient and what remedies to prescribe.

▼ A papyrus showing ancient Egyptian healing spells.

▲ These ancient Egyptian hieroglyphs spell out the word "doctor" or "physician."

The tradition of healers training with their families was also found in ancient China, where sons studied with their fathers. Like Egyptian doctors, professional Chinese healers were expected to be familiar with a range of medical texts giving advice on symptoms and remedies. However, in both countries only the rich were able to afford professional doctors, and most people must have relied on friends, family, and amateur healers for medical advice.

The same is true of classical Greece, where doctors were greatly respected. Medical schools flourished for the first time, although they were very different from those of today.

▲ An ancient Chinese doctor taking a pulse.

Greek physicians set up surgeries where they treated patients for a fee. The most famous medical school was on the island of Cos. Here the best-known doctor of all time, Hippocrates—the father of Western medicine—learned his trade. When he died his fame was so great people believed that the bees visiting the flowers on his grave made wax with special healing powers. Hippocrates had very specific ideas about doctors and their patients, which still form the basis of modern medicine today.

◄ A physician from the ancient Greek city of Athens at work in the early 2nd century AD.

▲ Hippocrates, who lived in ancient Greece, is considered the father of Western medicine.

The doctor's promise

Some of Hippocrates' ideas were gathered into the Hippocratic Oath—a series of promises that medical students had to make before they could begin their work. They promised to do everything in their power to help the sick, never to give a fatal poison to anyone, and never to tell anyone else about things they discussed in private with their patient.

At about the same time, doctors training in the Ayurvedic tradition in India had to make similar vows. The *Caraka Samhita*, a book written in AD 100, tells us that Ayurvedic doctors had to promise never to carry weapons, to speak the truth, to eat a vegetarian diet, and to strive to bring relief to their patients. These ideals were sound enough, but unfortunately doctors in the ancient world didn't know enough about medicine to succeed every time their help was needed. So by the Roman era, people were quite doubtful about how useful doctors could be.

Help for the rich—and the poor

There were no official examinations for doctors in ancient Greece or Rome. Students simply attached themselves to a teacher, and anyone could claim to be a doctor. For a long time in the Roman Empire almost all the doctors were immigrants from Greece, and many were slaves or ex-slaves. As time went by, the citizens of Rome became less afraid of the medical profession, and some doctors were even paid a fee by the civic authorities so that rich and poor alike could receive medical care. Most doctors relied on their reputation to attract patients, and those who did well could make large amounts of money.

▲ A 19th-century Ayurvedic healer in India.

▲ These pictures of a doctor's surgery in ancient Greece were painted on a vase.

This was also the case in Europe right up until the 1200s and 1300s. Most people couldn't afford to visit a doctor, but a whole range of healers offered cheaper alternatives. They included charmers, wise women, herbalists, and piss prophets who claimed they could make a diagnosis by looking at a patient's urine. Some modern scientists have even suggested that these herbalists and wise women had a better understanding of natural remedies than medieval doctors, who relied on old-fashioned medical texts. Through trial and error, folk healers discovered a whole range of effective painkillers, digestive aids, and soothing salves. Unfortunately, wise women were often confused with witches at this time and accused of doing harm rather than good.

▲ Healers in the Middle Ages collecting herbs for their medicines.

Over the last two hundred years, the governments of the world have gradually passed laws that have organized medicine and how it is practiced. Doctors undergo long training programs and have to pass many exams before they are allowed to treat patients. Most medicines are only available with a doctor's prescription, and most things modern doctors prescribe are unlikely to harm the patient. However, people still realize that going to see a doctor is not the only alternative if they fall ill, and today (as in medieval times) there are a whole range of therapists offering advice on diet, exercise, and herbal remedies.

▼ Medical students watching an operation in 1898.

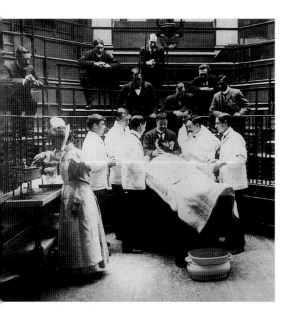

▶ Nowadays medical students go through a rigorous training program, with a lot of exams.

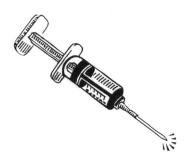

Prevention is better than cure
Can healthcare and hygiene limit disease?

HAVE YOU ever heard anyone say "prevention is better than cure"? People have always tried to find ways of preventing illness, especially in the past, when they might not have trusted their doctors to make them better if they fell ill. There are all sorts of ways to limit the effects of disease, and some of them are quite simple.

Clean clothes and healthy eating

The hot climate in Egypt encourages harmful bacteria that spread disease. The ancient Egyptians did not know about bacteria, but because of the heat wore loose clothing. This allowed their skin to breathe and prevented a build-up of bacteria. They also washed their clothes often—unlike people hundreds of years later in medieval Europe, who were a pretty stinky bunch.

Because the Nile River runs the length of Egypt it was easy to transport fresh fruit and vegetables from more fertile parts of the country to areas where

they were harder to grow. Even poor people in ancient Egypt ate a healthy, varied diet. Some ancient Egyptian houses have been found with wooden or stone seats with a removable bowl, which probably served as a kind of toilet. However, the typical Egyptian house, built of baked bricks and Nile mud, was infested by pests such as rats and fleas that spread disease.

▲ This wall painting from the tomb of Nebamun features an offering table piled with food. It shows what a varied, healthy diet the ancient Egyptians ate. On the table you can see wine jars, bread, meat, fruit, and vegetables.

▶ Egyptian paintings show the comfortable, cool clothing worn by ancient Egyptians.

▲ The Pont du Gard, a Roman aqueduct that carried fresh water into the city of Nemausus (modern Nîmes in France).

▼ A Roman sewer.

Clean water

The ancient Romans, who liked to organize their towns and cities, were the first to think about improving public health. They built public toilets, sewers to carry away waste, and aqueducts to bring in fresh water. The first aqueduct brought water into Rome in 312 BC. By AD 100 there were eight aqueducts carrying fresh water in tunnels and channels underneath the city streets. The water had to pass through settling tanks outside the city limits, so a lot of the harmful bacteria that cause diseases like dysentery would have been removed. Only the very wealthy could afford to have water piped directly into their houses, but a fresh water supply was only a short walk away for most Romans. Regular bathing also played an important part in Roman life. Most towns across the Roman Empire had at least one bath house, and entrance fees were cheap enough to allow even poorer Romans to make regular visits. The bath houses were places to get clean, to meet, to have a massage, and even sometimes to have medical treatments.

Even in this organized world, life was not perfect. Despite their long, straight roads it was still difficult for the Romans to transport goods. It was hard to make sure that all the citizens of the Empire ate a varied diet, including fresh fruit and vegetables. Food shortages were common, and in bad times Rome's poor were issued daily rations of corn to prevent them from starving. Building sewer systems in cities was a good idea, but there were times when the sewers overflowed, polluting rivers and spreading disease.

▼ This wall-painting shows a Roman party. Wealthy Romans ate a varied diet, but not all Romans were so lucky.

▲ People scramble to get away from a leper as they hear his bell.

Frightening illnesses

From the end of the fifth century AD the Roman Empire went into decline. Public health took a turn for the worse. In the medieval world, little was done to try to prevent disease, except in times of crisis. People were terrified of the rapid spread of diseases like the Black Death. In some cities, like Milan in Italy, victims were simply locked into their houses and left to die, for fear the plague should spread further. Leprosy was another disease that frightened medieval people, and lepers were forced to wear special clothing so that everyone would know they were infected. They also had to carry a handbell, which they rang to warn others they were approaching. Yet things were not completely bleak. The Christian Church played an important part in medieval life, and the church believed that it was its Christian duty to care for the sick, who might spread infection if they were cared for in the community. Many monasteries set up hospitals where people who were ill could be cared for. Monks also cultivated herb gardens so they had all the necessary ingredients for their medicines close at hand.

Overcrowding

Later on, from the 1700s onward, the Industrial Revolution led to a huge increase in the number of people living and working in cities. Living conditions were overcrowded, and children often had to work very long hours, just as their parents did. Many were poor and badly fed, and so they suffered from diseases like rickets and scurvy because they weren't getting enough vitamins and minerals from their diet. Dysentery and cholera—both of which are passed on by polluted water—were common, and people did not expect to live very long. Smallpox was also a huge problem, claiming hundreds of lives. One of the most important developments

CHOLERA DISTRICTS.

LOOSENESS of the BOWELS is the Beginning of CHOLERA.

Thousands of Lives may be saved by attending in Time to this Complaint, which should on no account be *neglected* by either Young or Old, in Places where the Disease prevails.

When CRAMPS IN THE LEGS, ARMS, or BELLY are felt, with LOOSENESS or SICKNESS AT STOMACH, when Medical Assistance is not at hand, *Three Tea-spoonsfull* of MUSTARD POWDER *in Half a Pint of warm Water*, or the same Quantity of warm Water with as much COMMON SALT as it will melt, should be taken as a Vomit; and after the Stomach has been cleared out with more warm Water, TWENTY-FIVE DROPS OF LAUDANUM should be taken in a small Glass of any agreeable Drink.

HEATED PLATES or PLATTERS to be applied to the BELLY and PIT of the STOMACH.

As Persons run considerable Risk of being infected by visiting those suffering from this Disease in crowded Rooms, it is most earnestly recommended that only such a Number of Persons as are sufficient to take care of the Sick be admitted into the Room.

Central Board of Health,
Council Office, Whitehall, 15th Feb. 1832.

W. MACLEAN, *Sec^y*.

◀ These instructions were displayed in 1832 to try and minimize the harmful effects of cholera.

in public health was the discovery that a vaccination could be used to protect people from catching smallpox.

Vaccination

Vaccination was the brainchild of an English doctor, Edward Jenner (1749–1823). He had noticed in his country surgery that farmers who suffered from cowpox (a much less serious disease) never caught smallpox afterward. In 1796 Jenner carried out experiments on an eight-year-old boy. He deliberately infected the boy with contagious matter from a cowpox pustule. He later tried to infect the boy with smallpox and—luckily for both doctor and patient—his theory proved correct. Jenner was not the first doctor to try to use this method—but he was the first to have widespread success with vaccination. Nowadays vaccination programs across the world have helped to control diseases like polio and typhus.

Over the years most countries have made all sorts of improvements in public health. Better sewage systems have been created, clean water supplies provided, hospitals built and most people—even in poorer countries—have access to some sort of medical care. It is hard for us to imagine what it must have been like to live at a time when death and disease were a part of everyday life.

▲ This cartoon shows Edward Jenner, the inventor of the smallpox vaccination, with some of his patients.

▼ These postcards from the early 20th century promote health care and hygiene.

DON'T BIND BABY UP TOO TIGHTLY.

DON'T FORGET TO WASH BABY NIGHT AND MORNING, AS CLEANLINESS MEANS HEALTH AND HAPPINESS.

ALWAYS put your own hand in the hot water first.

THE AFTER-GLOW OF AN IZAL BATH

IZAL KILLS GERMS

Charms, spells, and healing gods
Magic and religion in medicine

PREHISTORIC people didn't know the scientific reasons for illness, so they often blamed evil spirits or supernatural causes. Today some people still carry lucky charms and say prayers for sick relatives and friends.

Healing gods

Belief in magical cures and healing gods has been around since prehistoric times. Cave paintings in France show human figures, who may have been doctor priests, wearing animal masks and performing ritual dances. We think these early sorcerers used a mixture of charms, amulets, spells, and herbal medicines to heal the sick.

◄ Ancient Egyptians believed the Eye of Horus had special healing powers.

The civilizations of ancient Egypt, Greece, and Rome each created their own magical and religious ways of healing. In ancient Egypt, Horus and Imhotep were the gods of medicine. Like many ancient peoples the Egyptians believed that disease could be caused by demons and evil spirits, and the magical and medical papyri are full of spells and incantations for warding off evil and healing the sick.

In ancient Greece, Apollo was the god of healing. However, a cult also grew up around the doctor god Asklepios, the son of Apollo, and temples were built in his honor in Greek cities and towns. Patients slept in the temples in the hope that the god would send them a dream telling them how to cure their illness.

Imhotep (*above*) was worshipped as a god of medicine in ancient Egypt. (*below*) Asklepios became a god of medicine in ancient Greece and Rome.

▲ The human figure in this prehistoric cave painting may have been a medicine man or shaman, about 15,000 years ago.

Later on, the Romans adopted Asklepios (calling him Aesculapius). Romans made sacrifices to Aesculapius and held festivals celebrating the god. One of the temple rituals involved the patient being visited by a snake. Does the symbol of the snake curled round a staff look familiar? It is still used by pharmacists today. In the hope of being cured, people also left clay, wood, or stone models of the diseased parts of their bodies at the temples. Archaeologists have found large numbers of these models, including legs, arms, feet, eyes, and ears.

◀ This terracotta ear is one of the offerings left by Greek and Roman patients at healing shrines.

It is not so strange that people turned to magic and religion in a world where sickness and death were always around the corner, and ways of treating illness were often expensive and unreliable. In fact, people believed in evil spirits and magical cures all over the world. In Persia, Ahura Mazda, the god of light and good, was responsible for health and hygiene. In Arabia, jinn (evil spirits) were blamed for bringing sickness and death. The Chinese thought that sickness was brought by an evil wind and was cured by exorcising the evil spirits, or wearing charms and amulets.

Punishments

In medieval Europe, the church taught that illness and death were sent by God as punishments. Certain diseases such as leprosy were associated with sin. People made pilgrimages to the tombs of holy men and women where they left offerings of wax and metal models of parts of the human body. In some countries at this time people also thought that the king could help cure one disease simply by touching the sick person.

Miraculous cures, witchcraft, and sorcery were used to heal the sick in Europe until just over a century ago. In many parts of the world, such as Africa and Asia, healers still include traditional charms among their remedies. In the West, people continue to blame divine powers for certain illnesses.

▲ Scrofula was known as the "King's Disease." People believed it could be cured by the touch of a royal person (this is Queen Mary I).

Suffering from a toothache? Why not try one of our medieval cures? Take a piece of paper and write out on it three times "Jesus Christ, for mercy's sake, take away this toothache." Now fold the paper up very tightly and throw it on the fire. (Be careful to make sure that there is an adult around to help you!) If everything goes according to plan, your toothache should go away . . .

Why take a pill for every ill?
Lotions, potions, and herbal cures

TODAY, hospitals and pharmacies are filled with all kinds of drugs, pills, lotions, and creams. There is a treatment for most illnesses, and most are very easy to take. Modern drugs have been through a whole range of tests to make sure they don't have any harmful side effects. Sometimes with very strong drugs—such as those used to treat cancer—people have to accept that they may feel worse before the treatment makes them better.

Most modern pharmacies also have an herbal section, where people can buy remedies made from plants and herbs. Some people prefer to use herbal remedies rather than chemical medicines because they believe herbal cures heal the body more naturally. But where did all these medicines come from? And how did people find out which plants and chemicals cured each disease?

Mud and manure

People have been using medicines to cure disease for thousands of years. In fact, people in the past have used all kinds of weird and wonderful ingredients in their treatments. The ancient Egyptians used excrement to treat a whole range of diseases. They prescribed human excrement, and the excrement of crocodiles, pelicans, and lizards. They also used mud from the Nile River, granite, bile collected from wild animals, and metals in their medicines. It must have been very difficult to collect some of the ingredients— such as tortoise bile or pelican poo!

◄ A 19th-century advertisement for a pill to cure all ills.

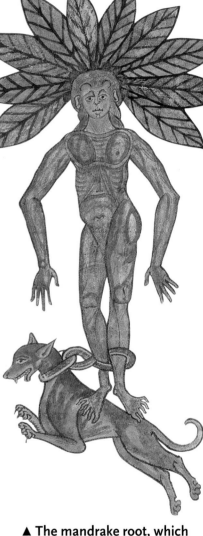

▲ The mandrake root, which resembles a human body, has been used in medicine since Roman times. In the Middle Ages dogs were used to pull up the root, because people believed that mandrakes would kill whoever uprooted them.

Pliny (AD 23-79), a famous Roman writer, collected together and listed a huge number of treatments. To cure a wild dog's bite he used badger, cuckoo, and swallow excrement, and mouse excrement was prescribed to sweeten sour breath. It is hard to imagine people believing that these cures really worked, but until the 18th century doctors continued to prescribe remedies that included very strange ingredients, such as pearls, woodlice, unicorn's horn, and frogs' eggs.

The salt, the sweet, and the sour

Some medicines people have taken in the past seem strange to us, but lots of old remedies were quite effective. Many are still used in some form by doctors today. The ancient Egyptians knew that opium, made from a type of poppy, was good for relieving pain. Opium is an ingredient of the modern drug morphine. Another remedy they used involved salt, which was rubbed on to cuts and sores and held in place with a bandage. Salt makes the cut sting, but

◄ Healing herbs found in the tomb of the Egyptian king Tutankhamun.

▲ Extracts from foxglove plants (*digitalis*) are still used to treat heart problems. But beware— foxglove plants are poisonous when growing!

▼ In China and Thailand medicine made from parts of the bodies of tigers are thought to have healing powers.

it has many healing properties. (Next time you get a cold sore or a sore throat, try gargling with salt water. You may be surprised at how effective it is.)

The legendary Chinese Emperor Shen Nung, the "father of Chinese medicine," who ruled China more than four and a half thousand years ago around 2737 BC, wrote an herbal manual that listed 365 herbs, poisons, and remedies. Not all of the emperor's treatments worked, but some are still used today. Good examples are kaolin, which is an excellent treatment for stopping diarrhea, and rhubarb, which has the opposite effect.

Buddhist monks in India were only allowed a few belongings, but their monastic rule stated that they had to carry five simple medicines wherever they went, including fresh butter, honey, and molasses. Early Indian herbal manuals teach about the healing properties of plants and, like the Chinese manuals, list hundreds of useful ingredients.

▲ In Roman times boxes like this one were used to hold medicines.

Sugar and spice

The ancient Greeks also used herbal manuals, although they were quite cautious about prescribing remedies more complicated than honey and water, or honey and vinegar. The most famous Greek pharmacologist, Dioscorides (c. AD 40–c. 90), wrote five books describing 600 medicinal plants. More adventurous Roman doctors traveled all over the Roman Empire learning about herbs and medicines from far-away places. Roman doctors knew that wine and vinegar could be used as antiseptics, and prescribed a range of soothing aloes and balsams. The sheer size of the Roman Empire meant that spices from far-off lands were available, at least to the wealthy.

D.I.Y. medicine

Exotic ingredients continued to be popular until the Middle Ages. Medieval doctors used the recipes

written down by Greek and Roman healers, and medieval apothecaries sold spices in their shops as well as medicines. Medieval healers also used a whole range of common-sense herbal cures, which had been passed down from generation to generation. These used free, locally growing plants rather than expensive foreign ingredients. It is amazing how much has been discovered about the healing powers of plants simply through trial and error, and until recently this practical do-it-yourself medicine was still used by country people.

▼ A page from a 12th-century herbal manual giving information about herbs and their healing properties.

▲ Comfrey is a traditional cure for sprains and bruises as well as broken bones.

Older people may remember having nasty cuts bound in spiders' webs to make them heal without a scar, or having broken limbs healed with the herb comfrey (also known as knitbone). Many modern medicines are based on remedies that have been used for hundreds of years—like aspirin, which comes from the bark of the willow tree.

However, not all doctors continued to prescribe natural, herbal cures. During the early 16th century the Swiss doctor Paracelsus (1493–1541) flew in the face of tradition, and started to prescribe chemicals such as mercury, antimony, arsenic, and sulphur. He is said to be the author of more than 600 works, although he claimed to scorn book learning and publicly burned the books of Galen and Hippocrates. He rejected many traditional medicines as old-fashioned, and encouraged the use of a whole range of new ingredients.

A moldy cure

Medicines continued to be improved, but it wasn't until the 20th century that really spectacular developments took place. After the First World War (1914-18) a Scottish doctor called Alexander Fleming (1881-1955), worked on wounds and skin infections. He discovered penicillin, a mold that killed the harmful bacteria that

▲ Alexander Fleming at work in his lab.

▼ Penicillin was the world's first known antibiotic. In 1928 Alexander Fleming discovered that penicillin could kill harmful bacteria.

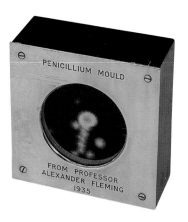

caused blood poisoning. Penicillin, along with a range of other antibiotics, didn't seem to have any harmful side effects, and antibiotics are still used to treat many illnesses and infections. In recent years, all sorts of treatments have become available, and modern doctors use a mixture of herbal and chemical medicines to treat everything from depression to cancer. But we still cannot cure the common cold.

The flash of the blade and the sound of the saw
Surgery through the ages

As long as there have been doctors there have been surgeons too. Surgeons treat illness or disease by operating: cutting, drilling, splinting, and stitching. An Indian book about medicine—the *Susruta Sanhita*, written more than 1,600 years ago—tells us that surgery is the oldest of the medical arts, and archaeologists think people probably used surgery at least 7,000 years ago!

A hole in the head

One of the most ancient operations is known to doctors today as trepanning. In trepanning, a hole is cut or drilled into the skull to ease a build-up of pressure inside. Skulls with these kinds of marks have been found in France, Egypt, South America, and the islands of the Pacific. Archaeologists can tell from the skulls they have found that some of the patients survived. It must have been a very painful operation, especially without an anesthetic. Modern doctors use anesthetics so that they can operate on patients without hurting them. A general anesthetic makes the patient fall soundly asleep so they don't feel anything. A local anesthetic stops the patient from feeling pain in a particular part of the body.

▲ A trepanned skull. The smooth edges of the holes show that the patient lived long enough for the wounds to heal.

Early surgeons at work

But what else could surgeons in the ancient world do? We know quite a lot about this because some of these healers wrote books describing their work. One of the oldest of these books comes from Egypt. It is written on papyrus and is more than 3,500 years old.

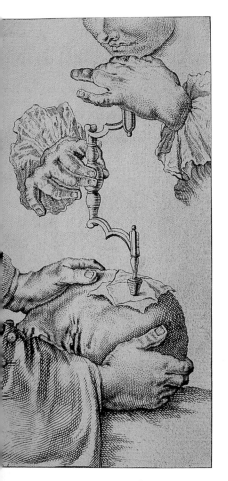

▲ This poor fellow is being trepanned.

▲ Arm bones from ancient Egypt. One has been broken and healed slightly crooked.

Magical and medical papyri tell us that Egyptian doctors were able to set broken bones in ox bone splints, wrapped in bandages soaked in resin—rather like having your leg put in a cast today. Looking at Egyptian mummies shows how well some of their fractures healed. The Egyptians also knew how to dress wounds and treat abscesses.

Archaeologists haven't been able to find any recognizable surgical instruments from ancient Egypt, but they have found many from the Roman Empire. The Romans were skilled at making surgical instruments out of metals such as copper, bronze, iron, and brass. As well as being able to set bones and treat abscesses, the Roman healers tackled a wide range of operations, from the amputation of arms and legs to the removal of in-grown eyelashes. Some were skilled eye surgeons.

New noses

As a general rule, that was as complicated as surgery got in the ancient world—with one strange exception. In India the punishment for one offense was for the guilty person's nose to be cut off. As a result Indian doctors came up with a way of rebuilding the nose using skin cut from the cheek and reed tubes to keep the nostrils open. This is one of the earliest known forms of plastic surgery!

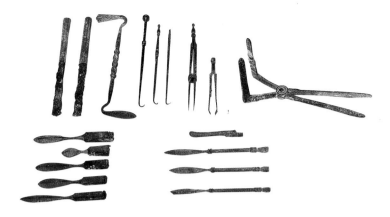

▲ These ancient Roman surgical instruments look surprisingly like modern surgical tools.

▲ An 18th-century microscope. The invention of the microscope in the 16th century enabled doctors to study micro-organisms for the first time.

▶ Surgery in the 12th century could be a nasty business.

Pain and danger

As medicine became more advanced surgery started to improve. However, surgery was a painful and dangerous business in a world without anesthetics and without any proper antiseptics. You probably know that if you get a cut, you need to clean it and put antiseptic cream on it to stop it from becoming infected. However, doctors didn't find out about the tiny organisms that cause blood poisoning and other infections until after the microscope was invented by Dutch eyeglass-makers in the late 16th century.

◄ Surgery in the 14th century.

► Medieval surgeons mistakenly believed that bleeding their patients would help them to get better.

Imagine what it must have been like to have a limb amputated in the past... the patient was held down by strong assistants. The skin was cut with a knife and the bone with a saw. In early amputations the wound was cauterized with hot oil to stop the bleeding. This continued to be the case until 1536, when a French army surgeon called Ambrose Paré (c.1510-90) perfected a system for tying off the ends of veins and arteries.

Without anesthetics, the shock of the pain could have killed the patient if infection didn't. Because of this danger, speed was extremely important, and doctors prided themselves on how quickly they could carry out operations. One well-known doctor, Robert Liston (1794–1847), worked in London in the early 1800s. He could amputate a leg in less than two minutes. After cutting the skin he would place the knife between his teeth so he could speedily take up his saw. But Robert Liston operated wearing dirty, bloody clothes, in a crowded operating theater filled with foul-smelling odors and the screams of the patient. Surgery could only advance after two important discoveries were made.

▼ Amputating a limb in the 16th century.

Serratura.

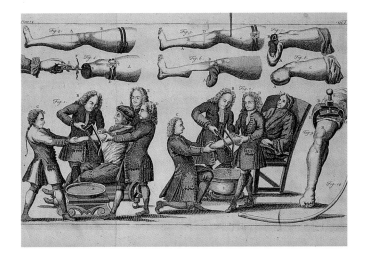

These diagrams were drawn in the 18th century to show the best way to amputate arms and legs.

Anesthetics arrive ...

The first discovery was that certain substances could be used to make patients drowsy. Doctors had experimented with hypnotism, but often had to resort to giving the patient large amounts of alcohol, so they woke up with a hangover on top of everything else! Crawford Long (1815–78), an American doctor, first used a chemical called ether to put patients to sleep in 1842. Later, Queen Victoria made use of a similar substance— chloroform—during the birth of one of her children. These early anesthetics were not perfect, but they still marked a vast improvement.

... and antiseptics

Then in 1865 a Scottish doctor, Joseph Lister (1827–1912), made another important discovery. He introduced the use of antiseptic carbolic acid to clean surgical instruments and dress wounds. He even sprayed a fine carbolic mist in the operating theater, which greatly reduced the risk of infection. Many more patients survived the operating theater after these discoveries were made. Today surgeons wear clean clothing, face masks, and disposable gloves. Conditions have improved so much in modern operating theaters that highly skilled surgeons can do anything from removing in-grown toenails to replacing the human heart.

▲ Joseph Lister and his assistants.

▼ A 21st-century operating theater.

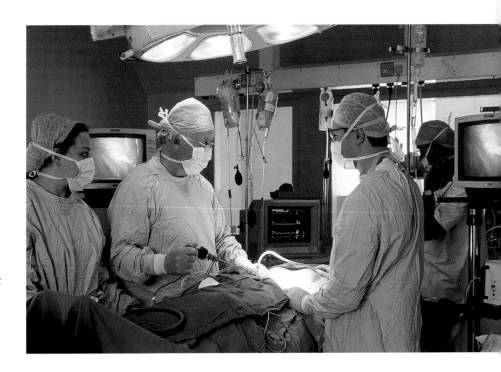

Deadly diseases
Catch them if you can!

MANY DISEASES were unknown to prehistoric people. In early times people found their food by hunting wild animals and gathering plants and nuts. Later, when people began to domesticate animals, they came into contact with all sorts of illnesses. Cows brought cowpox, which later became smallpox in human beings. Pigs and ducks gave us influenza, and horses brought the viruses that cause the common cold. Water polluted with animal wastes spread diseases like diphtheria, cholera, and whooping cough. Towns and cities provided the perfect environment for rats, fleas, and other pests that spread disease.

▲ A cartoon from the magazine *Punch* from 1858. The River Thames in London once carried all sorts of diseases in its polluted waters.

The people of the ancient Near East were the first to domesticate animals, and ancient Egyptian tomb paintings show that cattle were farmed in Egypt more than 5,000 years ago. Studying Egyptian mummies tells us that tuberculosis was already around in ancient Egyptian times. People caught tuberculosis from drinking infected cows' milk or eating infected meat. Some kinds of tuberculosis can damage the spine, so it's easy to tell whether an Egyptian mummy had the disease. Unfortunately, many other diseases kill without leaving any traces on the bones. So we can only find out about these illnesses when people in the past wrote about them.

▼ This painting from an Egyptian tomb shows ancient Egyptian farmers counting their herd of cattle.

▲ Trying anything to cure cholera.

▲ A medallion showing Aesculapius coming to the rescue of Roman plague victims in 295 BC.

Epidemics

We know that epidemics of diseases have occurred throughout history. A Greek historian records a plague—perhaps measles or smallpox—that killed a quarter of the Athenian army in 430 BC. The Romans also suffered from epidemics, and travelers could spread diseases far and wide across the huge Roman Empire. An unknown disease struck Rome in AD 165. The Roman army had been fighting in Mesopotamia (modern Iraq), and when the troops returned home they brought the sickness with them. The epidemic lasted 15 years and stretched all the way from Gaul to Persia, killing many thousands of Roman citizens.

Plague!

Then in AD 542 an even bigger epidemic broke out. It was probably bubonic plague— a disease carried by the fleas that live on rats. Roman doctors did not know much about the disease and so they had no effective way to treat it. Even the Roman Emperor Justinian (c. AD 482–565) became ill, although luckily for him he survived. The plague killed Roman officials and slaves alike. Hundreds of thousands died, and the epidemic may have been one of the things that contributed to the decline of the Roman Empire.

Bubonic plague struck again in the 14th century, when it was known as the Black Death. It was probably brought to Europe by Italian merchants returning from the Black Sea. Italian cities saw the first cases of the plague in 1347, and from Italy it spread across France, Germany, Holland, and England, killing more than a quarter of the population of Europe. Doctors at the time did not know that the disease was spread by micro-organisms. They thought the infection was caused by the wrath of God and carried in foul-smelling mists called miasmas. Doctors wore protective leather aprons and strange beak-like masks filled with sweet-smelling herbs, and they burned incense in the bedrooms of the sick in an attempt to drive out the disease.

▶ A 14th-century plague doctor in special protective clothing.

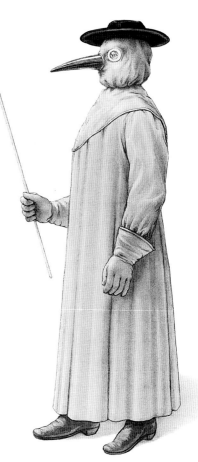

▲ We know now that fleas like this one carried plague.

▲ During times of plague, city dwellers buried their dead in huge pits outside the city limits.

Across Europe, cities struck by plague closed their gates to travelers. Orders were issued for all cats and dogs to be killed. But nothing the authorities did seemed to halt the spread of the plague. Terrified people looked for someone to blame, and Jews were accused of poisoning wells and deliberately spreading the plague. Many Jews were tortured or burned alive before Pope Clement VI declared that the Jews were innocent.

The Black Death ended in 1351, but in Europe bubonic plague continued to be a problem for hundreds of years. Officials did everything they could to limit the spread of plague. In many cities the sick were simply locked up in their houses and left to die. Huge pits were dug beyond the city limits to bury the bodies of the dead. Searchers were employed to go about and identify the houses where plague victims lived. Some families deliberately locked themselves in their homes, while others fled the cities. Those who remained took precautions not to come into contact with others, even paying for their food with money left in bowls of vinegar. Then the plague began to die out

► Coughs and sneezes really do spread diseases! This government poster is urging cold sufferers to be careful not to spread their germs to other people.

in Europe. Perhaps people became immune to the disease, or perhaps the rats who carried the fleas did. No one is quite sure why, but the plague left England, Italy, France, and Russia in the 18th century. The last great European plague epidemic was in Marseilles, France, in 1720, and the last epidemic in Asia and the United States was in the 1890s.

Flu and measles

Today you would be very surprised if a doctor said you were suffering from the plague. A more recent epidemic was a disease you probably associate with nasty winter weather and sore throats. It was an influenza epidemic,

aaaa...TISHOO

coughs and sneezes spread diseases

trap the germs in your HANDKERCHIEF

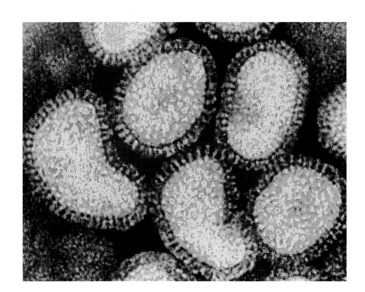

◄ An influenza virus seen through a microscope.

HIV can be treated

Take control - take the test

10,000 people in the UK do not know that they have HIV

10,000 people are not getting the help they need

which swept the world in 1918. It spread from Africa to the United States and Europe. Spanish flu, as it was called, killed 25 million people in six months—the most deadly epidemic since the Black Death. Sometimes seemingly harmless diseases can have devastating effects when people come into contact with them for the first time. The first Europeans to sail down the Amazon River in 1542 were practically immune to the effects of measles, but Amazonian Indians died in the hundreds when exposed to the disease.

But don't worry if you catch measles or flu. It's unlikely they will kill you off. In fact, since the Great Influenza Epidemic, there haven't been any disease disasters of this type. Living conditions across the world have improved, so people have better immune systems to fight disease. And immunization and treatment programs have brought diseases like polio and tuberculosis under

control. However, new diseases such as HIV, the virus that causes AIDS, can still cause fear and suffering. When the disease was first identified in the 1980s there was a great panic, and some frightened people claimed that the sickness was a punishment from God. Does that sound familiar?

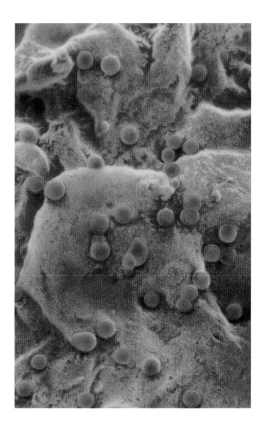

▲ New diseases, like AIDS, are developing all the time. We may have to deal with many more diseases in the future.

◄ A cell infected with the HIV virus. This virus causes the disease AIDS.

Endings or beginnings?
Ways of dealing with death

IN THE MODERN WORLD preventive medicine, better living conditions, and improved medical treatments enable most people to live long lives. But until the 20th century people didn't expect to live nearly as long. If you had lived over a hundred years ago, it is more than likely that by the age you are now, you would have lost some of your friends and family. This is still the case in many developing countries today.

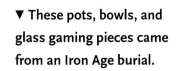

▲ This Iron Age warrior from Deal in eastern England was buried wearing his crown.

All over the world, from the last Ice Age—about 15,000 years ago—to the present day, people have developed ways of dealing with death. This is partly for practical reasons. Decomposing bodies are very smelly and can spread disease so, unless your community is on the move, dead bodies have to be disposed of by means such as burial or burning. Other rituals may have grown up to help the living with the grieving process. Losing somebody you love is very distressing. When it happens, having a set of rules and regulations to follow helps to draw people together in their time of need. It may also help grieving friends and relatives to believe that death is not the absolute end of that person's existence. The funeral ceremonies and burial practices of people in ancient Egypt, ancient Greece, Anglo-Saxon England, Viking Europe, and early America may be quite different from one another, but most of them have something in common—they show belief in the continuation of life after death.

Graves and grave goods

As far back as Neolithic times—from around 5000 BC—people were burying their dead in marked

▼ These pots, bowls, and glass gaming pieces came from an Iron Age burial.

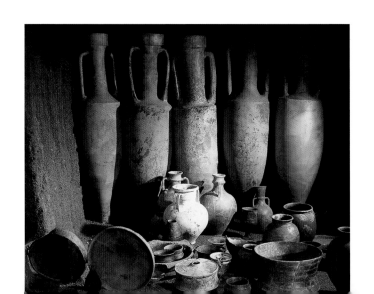

▶ A dead person faces the judgment of the gods in the ancient Egyptian "weighing of the heart" ceremony.

▼ The ancient Egyptians mummified animals as well as people. Cats like this one were sacred to the goddess Bastet.

▶ Don't lose your head! This protective mummy-mask belonged to an ancient Egyptian priest.

graves, with food, weapons and other useful items the dead person could take with them to the afterlife. We know this because archaeologists have discovered many Neolithic graves and investigated their contents. But the grave goods found in Neolithic burials are not nearly as spectacular as those found in the tombs of the ancient Egyptians. Egyptian graves even contained instructions on how to deal with the afterlife, written down in *The Book of the Dead*,

▶ This amulet is a heart scarab in the shape of the sacred scarab beetle. Scarab amulets were placed in the wrappings of Egyptian mummies as a protection.

which included information on how to avoid injuries such as being bitten by a snake or dying for a second time. The ancient Egyptians believed it was important for the body of a dead person to reach the afterlife intact. They developed mummification so that the body could be preserved and placed in the tomb wrapped in bandages and encased in a protective coffin. One of the worst things that could happen to an Egyptian person in the afterlife was losing his or her head, so many mummies wore protective masks as well.

Ferry across the River Styx

The ancient Egyptians were not the only ones to believe in an afterlife. The ancient Greeks thought that a dead person had to travel to an underworld ruled by the god Hades and guarded by the three-headed dog, Cerberus. To reach the underworld, the dead person had to cross over the River Styx, paying a fee to Charon the ferryman. Another river flowing through the underworld was the River Lethe. The Greeks believed that by drinking from the waters of Lethe, the river of forgetfulness, people lost the memory of everything that had happened to them before they died.

Ship burials

Ships and boats feature in the funerary rituals of other cultures too. One famous ship burial is at Sutton Hoo in eastern England. An Anglo Saxon king—perhaps the sixth century king Raedwald—was laid in a great sea-going ship and a huge mound of earth was raised over it, burying the ship completely. It was not uncovered until 1939.

▲ This ancient Greek pot shows Charon, the ferryman who took the dead across the River Styx to the underworld.

▼ A Viking sword found buried in a warrior's grave.

▲ A Viking warrior being welcomed into Valhalla.

In the Viking world it was important for warriors to fight bravely and honorably to make sure they would be allowed to enter the great hall of Valhalla when they died. Valhalla was the Viking paradise. Here warriors who had died on the battlefield feasted from dawn to dusk every day, completely healed of their wounds. The bodies of important kings or warriors were sometimes buried inside a longboat or Viking ship, with farming tools, kitchen utensils, food, and drink.

Funeral pyres

The Vikings and other peoples also disposed of dead warriors and kings by building a funeral bonfire, called a pyre, and burning the body.

◄ The helmet and coins were among the grave goods discovered in a sixth-century ship burial at Sutton Hoo in England.

and it was banned in 1829. However, the last person to commit sati in India did so in 1987.

Sati was banned partly because the widows were taking their own lives. Suicide is frowned upon by most religions, and this plays an important part in modern arguments about euthanasia, or assisted death. Some people now argue that we are living too long, and that modern medicine can prolong life past the point where it is enjoyable. Euthanasia gives patients the right to request that their life be ended should their health worsen. This could mean turning off a life-support machine, or giving a lethal dose of pain-killing drugs. A large number of people are in favor of euthanasia, but many others are not. Euthanasia is still illegal everywhere except Japan, Columbia, the Netherlands and the state of Oregon. Many doctors feel that it goes against their principles of only using their knowledge to help the sick.

In some cases the dead man's widow was expected to throw herself on to the burning pyre to join her husband in death. This ritual was once part of the Hindu way of life in India. There, widowhood was shameful and some women preferred to die rather than face life without a husband. Widows did not have to commit suicide to join their husbands in death, but it was considered very brave and praiseworthy to do so. Sometimes the widow would come to the funeral wearing full bridal make-up and clothes, as if she were going to marry her husband again. This practice was known in India as suttee or sati,

◄ This memorial stone commemorates a widow who committed sati in the 18th century. The upturned hand was a symbol often found on sati stones.

What's the alternative?
Complementary medicine in the Western world

AN ALTERNATIVE therapy is one that uses healing techniques different from those of conventional doctors. Alternative therapies have gained in popularity in recent years, but they are not an entirely new development. People have been complaining for a long time that conventional medicine is narrow-minded and doesn't take into account all the treatments available. In fact, some people believe that conventional Western medicine is sick itself, because it relies on chemicals and bold surgical methods rather than natural cures.

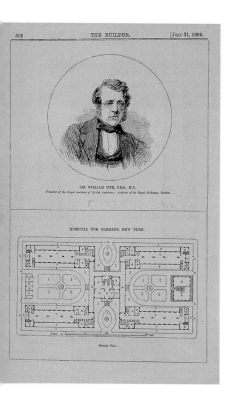

▲ A 19th-century plan for a homeopathic medical college in New York City.

A kick-start cure

One of the first alternative therapies to become really popular was homeopathy. It was invented in the early 1800s. Homeopathy works on the theory that one disease drives out another. The body of a sick person shows symptoms of the illness. Homeopathic treatments give the sick person a controlled amount of something that causes symptoms similar to the illness. This starts up the body's own healing ability. So somebody with insomnia (inability to sleep) and trembling might be prescribed a very small dose of coffee. Coffee stimulates the body and drinking strong coffee at night can stop people sleeping. So in theory a small dose of coffee should trigger the body's natural defenses and kick-start the healing process.

Straight spines

Osteopathy and chiropractic are therapies that grew up in the later 1800s. Both osteopaths and chiropractors concentrate on the spine, manipulating the bones and joints and popping bones that are out of line back into place.

▼ An osteopath treating a patient.

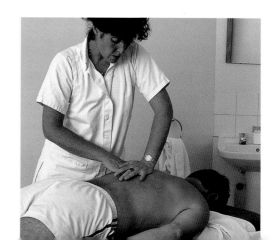

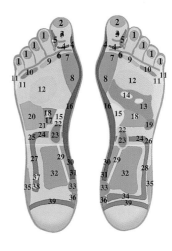

◀ Acupuncture treatment has become popular with people all around the world.

▼ A diagram of pressure points and energy flows in the human body, from a Thai manuscript.

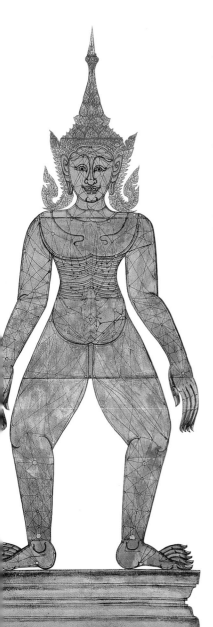

Chinese needles

One of the most popular alternative therapies today is acupuncture. This is a technique originally developed by the Chinese some 5,000 years ago. It works on the principle that energy flows through channels in the body and using special pressure points can affect the flow of energy. The acupuncturist puts very fine needles into the pressure points that relate to particular illnesses or parts of the body to unblock the energy flow and heal the patient.

Toe hold

Reflexology also uses pressure points, but in reflexology the points are all on the foot. The reflexologist finds out what the patient's symptoms are and massages the feet in the relevant place. Next time you get a headache, try massaging your big toes all around the edges and on the sole. You might find it as helpful as taking an aspirin.

Today there are almost as many alternative therapists as there are conventional doctors. Many doctors actually refer some of their patients to an alternative therapist for treatment. Alternative therapies are popular in countries such as Britain, France, the United States, and Canada, where one in five people uses meditation, massage, acupuncture, hypnosis, or other treatments. Recently in Britain the British Medical Association recommended that acupuncture should be made freely available on the National Health Service. In hospital wards that look after people who are dying it is not unusual to find nurses using aromatherapy or reflexology to ease their patients' suffering. Slowly but surely, conventional Western medicine is opening its eyes to the wide range of therapies that can help the sick.

▲ This diagram shows the reflexology pressure points on the soles of the feet.

What now and whatever next?
The future of medicine

DURING the last hundred years medicine has made huge advances. Surgery was once difficult and dangerous, but now doctors can remove and replace organs—even the heart— in safe, antiseptic operating theaters. The new heart can then be checked and controlled with an artificial device called a pacemaker. Tiny babies, born weeks early, can be kept alive in special incubators until they are big enough to survive on their own. And in Intensive Care units, people whose hearts and lungs have stopped working can be hooked up to machines that will pump blood and breathe for them.

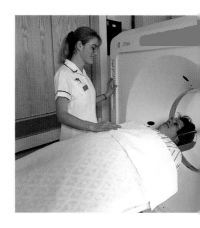

▲ A patient entering a CAT scanner.

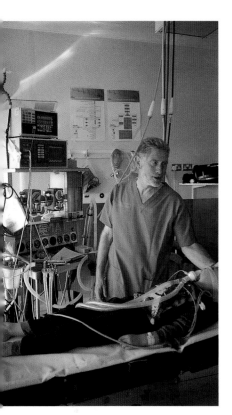

▲ An anesthetist looking after a patient in a modern operating theater.

X rays and CAT scans allow doctors to see detailed pictures of the inside of the human body without having to cut patients open. In fact, it's thanks to CAT scans and X rays that palaeopathologists know so much about the insides of ancient mummies. And scientists can make artificial replacements for parts of the body that go wrong, such as hip joints and heart valves.

Looking forward

What does the future hold? One of the important things to remember is that most of these exciting developments are only happening in wealthy countries. Many people in the developing world still suffer from inadequate health care, so one thing we could hope for is that better medical care will be available to everyone.

In the developed world doctors can carry out some operations through a very small hole in the body. This is called keyhole surgery and the surgeon uses tiny cameras, lasers, and robots. Doctors hope to carry out many more operations this way.

As medicine becomes more advanced, people are living longer. Doctors are having to deal with more of the diseases that come with old age. These include rheumatism and arthritis (diseases that make the joints sore and swollen) and Alzheimer's disease (which can make people forgetful and confused).

New diseases

New diseases, such as AIDS, are developing all the time. And there is still no cure for many older diseases such as multiple sclerosis and some forms of cancer. So scientists are searching for new remedies. One place they are looking for help is in our genes—the complex pattern books inside our bodies that decide what we look like and what inherited diseases we may have. Scientists are currently experimenting on copying (cloning) and altering genes.

▼ Is this how surgery might look in the future?

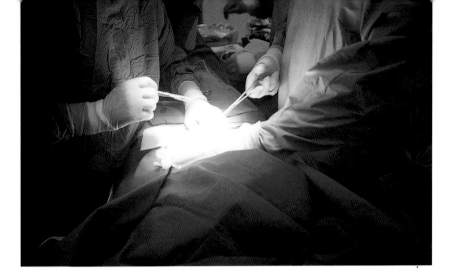

▲ Surgery has come a long way in the last 200 years, and new surgical techniques are developing all the time.

Dolly the sheep was the first ever cloned animal. Some genetically altered crops can resist plant diseases.

However, genetic engineering has been criticized for taking medicine too far. There are many questions for modern medicine. Should doctors try to prolong life indefinitely? Should they be allowed to tamper with our genetic make-up? Or might this start off a chain of unpredictable and perhaps dangerous events?

What do you think?

▼ A sweater made from the wool of Dolly, the first genetically engineered sheep. In the early 1990s it would have been impossible to clone a sheep. What will the next ten years bring?

What now and whatever next? ■ **39**

Index

aqueducts 15
acupuncture 37
Aesculapius *see* Asklepios
AIDS 19, 31, 39
alternative medicine 36–37
amputations 26, 27
amulets 18, 33
anatomy 6, 7, 8
anesthetics 24, 26, 27
antibiotics 23
antiseptics 25, 27
Asklepios, Greek and
    Roman god of medicine
    18, 19, 29
Ayurvedic medicine 12
Black Death 16, 29, 30
bubonic plague 29
Burke, William (1792–1829),
    grave-robber 9
burial 32, 33, 34
cancer 20
carbolic acid 27
CAT scan 38
Chinese medicine 11, 19, 21
chloroform 27
cholera 16, 28
comfrey 22, 23
diet 14, 15

Dioscorides (AD 40–90),
    Greek pharmacologist 22
disease 29–31, 38
dissection 6, 7, 8
Dolly, the cloned sheep 38
dysentery 16
Egypt 14, 28
Egyptian mummies 28, 33
epidemics 29, 30
ether 27
euthanasia 35
evil spirits 19
Fleming, Alexander
    (1881–1995),
    discovered penicillin 23
funeral pyres 34
Galen (AD 129–216),
    Greek doctor 7
genes and genetic
    engineering 38
Hare, William
    (c.1790–c.1860),
    grave-robber 9
herbal medicine 20, 21, 22
Hippocrates
    (c.490–c.375 BC),
    Greek doctor 7, 11, 12
homeopathy 36

hygiene 14, 15
Imhotep, Egyptian god
    of medicine 18
Indian medicine 24
influenza 28, 30, 31
Jenner, Edward (1749–1823),
    pioneered vaccination 17
keyhole surgery 38
leprosy 16, 19
Lister, Joseph (1827–1912),
    first to use antiseptics 27
Liston, Robert (1794–1847),
    surgeon 26
Long, Crawford
    (1815–1878), first to use
    anesthetics 27
magic 18, 19
mandrake 20
measles 31
medical exams 12, 13
Medieval medicine 13, 16, 22
microscopes 25
monasteries
    and medicine 16
opium 21
osteopathy 36
Paracelsus (1493–1541),
    Swiss doctor 23

Paré, Ambrose (1510–1590),
    French surgeon 26
penicillin 23
plague 29, 30
Pliny (AD 23–79), Roman
    writer 21
reflexology 37
Roman medicine 21, 22, 25
sati 35
scrofula 19
Shen Nung, emperor of
    China (c.2737 BC) 21
ship burials 34
smallpox 16, 17, 28
Spanish flu 31
surgery 24–27, 38, 39
surgical instruments 25
Susruta Sanhita, Indian
    medical book 24
Sutton Hoo ship
    burial 34, 35
trepanning 24
tuberculosis 28, 31
vaccination 17
Viking burials 34
X rays 38

Further reading

For children

3-D Kid: A Life-Size, Pop-up Guide to Your Body and How It Works,
    by Roger Culbertson (W.H. Freeman, 1995)
Eyewitness: Human Body, by Steve Parker (DK, 1999)
Eyewitness: Medicine, by Steve Parker (DK, 2000)
The Human Body, edited by Charles Clayman
    (Dorling Kindersley, 1995)
Incredible Body, by Stephen Biestly (Dorling Kindersley, 1998)
The Incredible Human Body, by Frances R. Balkwill and Rolph
    Mic (Sterling, 1998)

For adults

*Of Greatest Benefit to Mankind: A Medical History of Humanity
    from Antiquity to the Present*, by Roy Porter
    (HarperCollins, 1997)
Ancient Egyptian Medicine, by John F. Nunn,
    (British Museum Press 1996)
Doctors and Diseases in the Roman Empire, by Ralph Jackson
    (British Museum Press, 1988)
Medicine's 10 Greatest Discoveries, by Mayer Friedman
    & Gerald W. Friedland (Yale University Press, 2000)
History of Medicine, by Roberto Margotta (Hamlyn, 1996)
Medicine and Society in Later Medieval England, by Carole
    Rawcliffe (Sutton Publishing, 1995)
Wisdom, Memory and Healing, by Gabrielle Hatfield
    (Sutton Publishing, 1999)

Family Name

Date

Our
FAMILY

SHARED MOMENTS, MEMORIES,
AND TRADITIONS.

AMILY

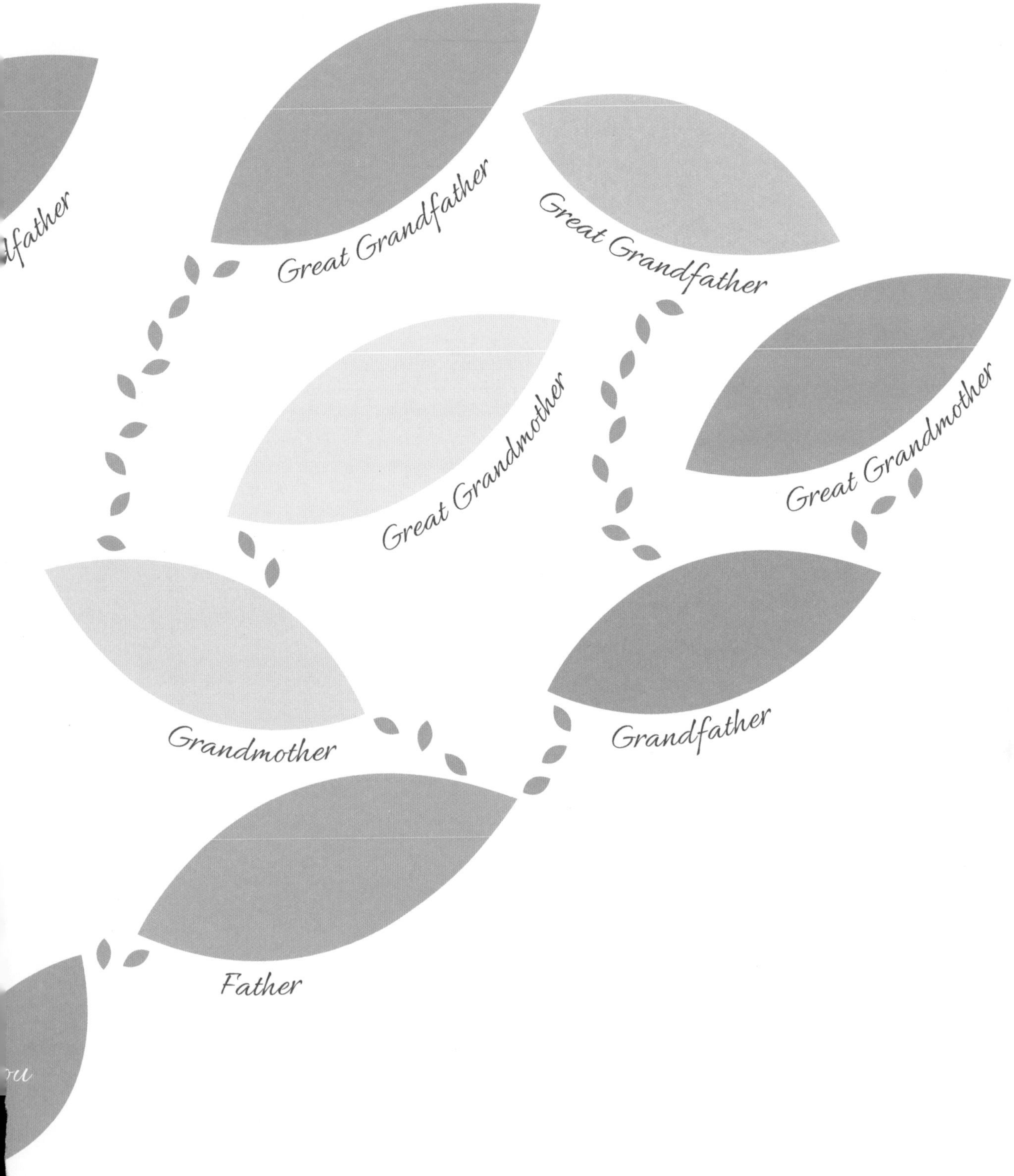

Great Grandfather

Great Grandfather

Great Grandfather

Great Grandmother

Great Grandmother

Grandmother

Grandfather

Father

Contents

Introduction

Letters, journals, photo albums, and scrapbooks are rare and invaluable links to the past. They are more precious still when written by your own grandparents, great grandparents, or distant relatives. What were their stories, their hopes, and their passions? Who did they love?

Have you ever discovered a journal or a letter written by an ancestor that gave you new insight into your family's history? If so, you will know that the value of such records cannot be overestimated. If you never had the good fortune to know the history of your ancestors, this is your opportunity to begin a tradition. This keepsake book may be a lasting heirloom for your descendants, who will want to know about you and your family, your hopes, and your history.

Fill in the first chapter of the keepsake book so that your family will know all about your relatives and ancestors. You may then write your own story, using the chapters as a personal journal or a letter to your loved ones. Present the finished book to your children, so they will know their family intimately. The journal may be passed on to your grandchildren, and on through the generations. You are not only documenting a personal memoir; you are creating an invaluable heirloom for generations to come.

Genealogy Resources

Here are some useful genealogy resources to help get you started as
you compile your family's unique history.

National Genealogical Society (NGS)
www.ngsgenealogy.org

The WorldGenWeb Project
www.worldgenweb.org

The USGenWeb Project
www.usgenweb.org

The Library of Congress
www.loc.gov

The U.S. National Archives and Records Administration
www.nara.gov

National Institute on Genealogical Research
www.rootsweb.com/~natgenin/

Tracing

Our Roots

Place photo here

All About Me

My full name is _____

This is the language from which our last name originates _____

In this language, our last name means _____

_____

Our ancestors spelled and pronounced our last name like this _____

_____

I was born in this city and state _____

My birthday is _____

I was born at this location _____

at this time _____

Here is a story that my parents told me about my birth _____

_____

_____

This is the story behind my first name _____

_____

_____

My nickname is _____

It was given to me by _____

because _____

_____

Place photo here

Place photo here

Place photo here

Place photo here

Place photo here

Place photo here

Place photo here

My Maternal Grandparents

My grandmother's full name is _____

She was born in this location _____

at this time _____

My grandmother is _____ generation American.

I called her _____

and this is the story behind the name _____

_____

This is a special memory I have about my grandmother _____

_____

_____

Place photo here

Place photo here

My grandfather's full name is _____

He was born in this location _____

at this time _____

My grandfather is _____ generation American.

I called him _____

and this is the story behind the name _____

_____

This is a special memory I have about my grandfather _____

_____

_____

Place photo here

My Paternal Grandparents

My grandmother's full name is _____

She was born in this location _____

at this time _____

My grandmother is _____ generation American.

I called her _____

and this is the story behind the name _____

_____

This is a special memory I have about my grandmother _____

_____

_____

My grandfather's full name is _____

He was born in this location _____

at this time _____

My grandfather is _____ generation American.

I called him _____

and this is the story behind the name _____

_____

This is a special memory I have about my grandfather _____

_____

_____

Place photo here

My Parents

My mother's full name is _____

She was born in this location _____

at this time _____

My mother is _____ generation American.

This is a story my mother told me about her childhood _____

_____

_____

_____

Place photo here

Place photo here

Place photo here

My father's full name is _____

He was born in this location _____

at this time _____

My father is _____ generation American.

This is a story my father told me about his childhood _____

_____

_____

_____

Place photo here

Place photo here

Place photo here

Place photo here

Place photo here

Place photo here

17

Brothers and Sisters

I am the _____ child.

I have _____ brothers and _____ sisters.

Their names and birthdays are _____

_____

_____

These are the names and birthdays of their spouses and children _____

_____

_____

_____

When we were little, we would squabble about _____

_____

_____

This is the activity that I most enjoy sharing with my siblings _____

_____

_____

Some other special sibling memories are _____

_____

_____

Place photo here

Place photo here

Place photo here

My Other Half

My spouse's nickname is _____,

but this is the pet name I use _____

My spouse was born in this location _____

on this date _____

This is the story of our marriage proposal _____

_____

_____

We were married at this location _____

on this date _____

Here is a description of our wedding _____

_____

_____

This is where we spent our honeymoon _____

_____

_____

My fondest memory of my first year of marriage _____

_____

_____

Place photo here

My Spouse's Parents

My mother-in-law's full name is _____

She was born in this location _____

at this time _____

She is _____ generation American.

This is a story my mother-in-law tells about her childhood _____

_____

_____

_____

This is the best advice my mother-in-law gave us _____

_____

_____

Here is what we admire most about my mother-in-law _____

_____

_____

My father-in-law's full name is _____

He was born in this location _____

at this time _____

He is _____ generation American.

This is a story my father-in-law tells about his childhood _____

_____

_____

_____

This is the best advice my father-in-law gave us _____

_____

_____

Here is what we admire most about my father-in-law _____

_____

_____

Place photo here

Place photo here

Place photo here

Place photo here

Place photo here

Place photo here

Place photo here

My Spouse's Maternal Grandparents

The full name of my spouse's grandmother is _____

She was born in this location _____

at this time _____

She is _____ generation American.

My spouse called her _____

and this is the story behind the name _____

_____

Here is my spouse's favorite memory about this grandparent _____

_____

_____

Place photo here

Place photo here

The full name of my spouse's grandfather is _____

He was born in this location _____

at this time _____

He is _____ generation American.

My spouse called him _____

and this is the story behind the name _____

_____

Here is my spouse's favorite memory about this grandparent _____

_____

_____

My Spouse's Paternal Grandparents

The full name of my spouse's grandmother is _____

She was born in this location _____

at this time _____

She is _____ generation American.

My spouse called her _____

and this is the story behind the name _____

_____

Here is my spouse's favorite memory about this grandparent _____

_____

_____

Place photo here

Place photo here

The full name of my spouse's grandfather is _____

He was born in this location _____

at this time _____

He is _____ generation American.

My spouse called him _____

and this is the story behind the name _____

_____

Here is my spouse's favorite memory about this grandparent _____

_____

_____

Place photo here

Place photo here

Place photo here

30

Place photo here

Place photo here

Place photo here

Place photo here

My Little Ones

My children's names and birthdays are _____

_____

_____

Here is a special memory about each of my children's births _____

_____

_____

_____

_____

My Grandkids

My grandchildren's names and birthdays are _____

_____

_____

My grandchildren call me _____

This is the story behind the name _____

_____

The most wonderful part of being a grandparent is _____

_____

_____

Place photo here

Through the Generations

This is a dominant family trait that every parent in my family hopes to pass on _____

_____

_____

_____

People often think my children resemble me in these ways _____

_____

_____

_____

This is a dominant physical feature in my family _____

_____

_____

_____

I am like my mother because _____

_____

_____

I am like my father because _____

_____

Place photo here

Place photo here

Place photo here

Place photo here

Place photo here

Place photo here

Place photo here

Place photo here

Place photo here

38

Childhood
Stories

Home

I grew up in _____

and lived there for _____ years.

Here is a description of my house and yard _____

_____

This is what my childhood bedroom looked like _____

_____

Here is a description of the neighborhood where I grew up _____

_____

These are the shops and restaurants I loved to visit when I was little _____

_____

Place photo here

Place photo here

Place photo here

Place photo here

My Friends

My best friend growing up was _____

Here is the story of how we met _____

_____

We most enjoyed playing these games _____

_____

When I was growing up, the most popular game to play with friends was _____

_____

I am still in touch with these childhood friends _____

_____

Here is a story my friends like to tell about me _____

_____

My Pets

These are the pets I had growing up _____

_____

Here are the stories behind my pets' names _____

_____

_____

The funniest story I remember about one of my pets is _____

_____

_____

As a child, I had these responsibilities when it came to our family pets _____

_____

_____

Place photo here

Place photo here

Entertaining Moments

My parents played these records _____

_____

My family and I watched these television shows _____

_____

and listened to these radio programs _____

_____

My favorite bedtime story was _____

_____

It was about _____

_____

This was the most popular movie when I was a child _____

_____

The top movie stars back then were _____

_____

It cost _____ to go to the movies.

When I was a child, this is what my family and I did for fun _____

_____

Political Point of View

When I was born, the president was _____

The country's top concerns were _____

_____

These were all the presidents who served during my lifetime _____

_____

_____

_____

This is one significant international or national event that I remember from my

childhood _____

_____

When I heard the news, I was _____

_____

I lived through this war when I was a child _____

_____

This is how the country's involvement in this war shaped my life _____

_____

_____

_____

To Be a Kid Again

This is my earliest memory _____

_____

_____

My fondest childhood memory is _____

_____

_____

If I could relive one event during my childhood, it would be _____

_____

This is how we dressed when I was a kid _____

_____

_____

I received _____ for allowance as a child.

I spent my money on _____

_____

As a child, my hero was _____

_____

I looked up to this person because _____

_____

Place photo here

Place photo here

Place photo here

Place photo here

Place photo here

Place photo here

The Teen Scene

Every generation of teens has a nickname, like Bobby-soxers and Generation X. The

nickname for my generation was _____

Here's a description of me as a teenager _____

_____

This is how I felt about the way I looked _____

_____

I started dating when I was _____ years old.

Here is a description of a typical date _____

_____

My curfew was _____

Place photo here

Place photo here

This is the story of the first time I fell in love _____

_____

I spent my money on _____

_____

My favorite bands and entertainers were _____

_____

When I was a teenager, these were the popular places to hang out _____

_____

Here are some of the phrases that teenagers used when I was growing up _____

_____

School Days

 # Elementary School

The name of my elementary school was _____

It had _____ grades and _____ students.

This is how I got to school each morning _____

_____

This is how children were disciplined when I was in grade school _____

_____

My favorite elementary school teacher was _____

This teacher was special because _____

_____

My favorite subjects in elementary school were _____

_____

My least favorite subjects were _____

_____

I was this type of student in elementary school _____

_____

Here is a description of how I dressed in school _____

_____

I started to get homework in this grade _____

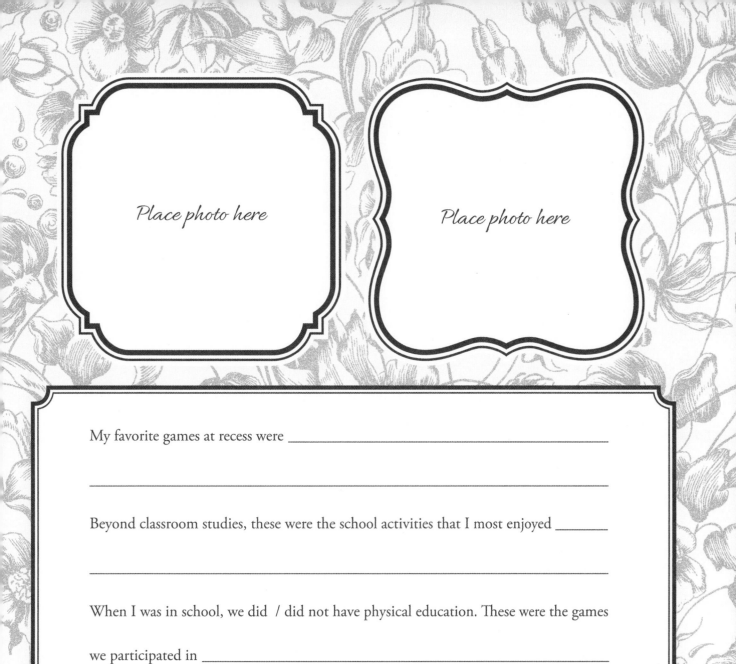

Place photo here

Place photo here

My favorite games at recess were _____

_____

Beyond classroom studies, these were the school activities that I most enjoyed _____

_____

When I was in school, we did / did not have physical education. These were the games

we participated in _____

_____

When I was in school, we did / did not have music and art education.

This was my favorite creative activity _____

_____

Here is a description of lunchtime at my school _____

_____

Reaching Higher

This was the name of my high school _____

There were _____ students in my graduating class.

I got to school each day by _____

_____

The high school teacher who most influenced me was _____

because _____

_____

My favorite subjects in high school were _____

_____

My least favorite subjects were _____

_____

Place photo here

Place photo here

I was this type of student _____

_____

When I was in high school, I had to take these classes that are no longer mandatory

today (like Home Economics or Shop) _____

_____

In these classes, I learned _____

_____

This is how I normally dressed for school _____

_____

I did / did not participate in high school sports.

These were my favorite sports _____

Beyond classroom studies, I was involved in these school activities _____

_____

I normally ate lunch with _____

and we talked about _____

I did / did not attend my high school prom.

The prom's theme song was _____

Here is a description of a school dance _____

_____

Place photo here

Place photo here

Place photo here

Place photo here

Place photo here

Place photo here

Ivy-Covered Walls

I attended this college _____

for these years _____

I chose to attend this college because _____

_____

Tuition was _____

My family paid for tuition by _____

Here is a description of the campus _____

_____

My major was _____

I selected this major because _____

The professor that most influenced my life decisions was _____

This professor influenced me because _____

_____

The one class that really opened my eyes and set the wheels in motion toward bigger

things was _____

_____

because _____

_____

I did / did not live in the dormitory. Here is a description of my living arrangements

_____

_____

My first roommate was _____

Beyond classroom studies, I participated in these activities _____

_____

This is what my friends and I did for fun _____

_____

_____

Looking back, the best part of my college days was _____

_____

_____

Family

Holidays

Our Traditions

These are the holidays that we celebrate with a big dinner every year _____

_____

_____

_____

We usually share these dinners with _____

_____

_____

_____

We always serve _____

_____

_____

_____

This is my favorite holiday memory _____

_____

_____

_____

_____

Place photo here

Place photo here

Place photo here

63

Wonderful Wintertime Holidays

This is the wintertime holiday that my family looks forward to _____

_____

We share this holiday with _____

_____

on this day _____

My favorite childhood memory or story about this holiday is _____

_____

_____

The oldest family tradition associated with this holiday is _____

_____

Place photo here

Place photo here

This tradition was started by _____

_____

because _____

_____

This holiday has special meaning for my family because _____

_____

This is what the adults most enjoy about this holiday _____

_____

This is what the kids most enjoy about this holiday _____

_____

These are our traditions when it comes to giving gifts _____

_____

_____

This is what the gifts were like when I was young _____

_____

_____

This is how gift-giving has changed over time _____

_____

_____

Another holiday that is important to my family is _____

_____

These family members traditionally gather for this holiday _____

_____

_____

We celebrate at this location _____

_____

A favorite childhood memory or story about this holiday is _____

_____

_____

Place photo here

Place photo here

When it comes to this holiday, the traditions that I most want to pass along to the next

generation are _____

_____

_____

This is the special food that I associate with this holiday _____

_____

_____

_____

Place photo here

Place photo here

Place photo here

Place photo here

Place photo here

Place photo here

Favorite Holiday Recipe

Favorite Holiday Recipe

Favorite Holiday Recipe

_____

_____

_____

_____

_____

_____

_____

_____

_____

_____

_____

_____

_____

_____

_____

_____

Favorite Holiday Recipe

Place photo here

Place photo here

Place photo here

74

Place photo here

Place photo here

Place photo here

Favorite Holiday Recipe

Favorite Holiday Recipe

Favorite Holiday Recipe

Favorite Holiday Recipe

Place photo here

Place photo here

Place photo here

Place photo here

Place photo here

Place photo here

Traditions and Folklore

Vacation Memories

This is what family vacations were like when I was a child _____

_____

_____

While growing up, my family returned to this particular vacation spot again and again

_____

_____

My most special memory of this place is _____

_____

My favorite vacation I took with my own family is _____

_____

My most special memory of this trip is _____

_____

_____

This is a vacation-related tale that my family loves to tell _____

_____

_____

_____

_____

Place photo here

Place photo here

Place photo here

Place photo here

Place photo here

Place photo here

Place photo here

Our F

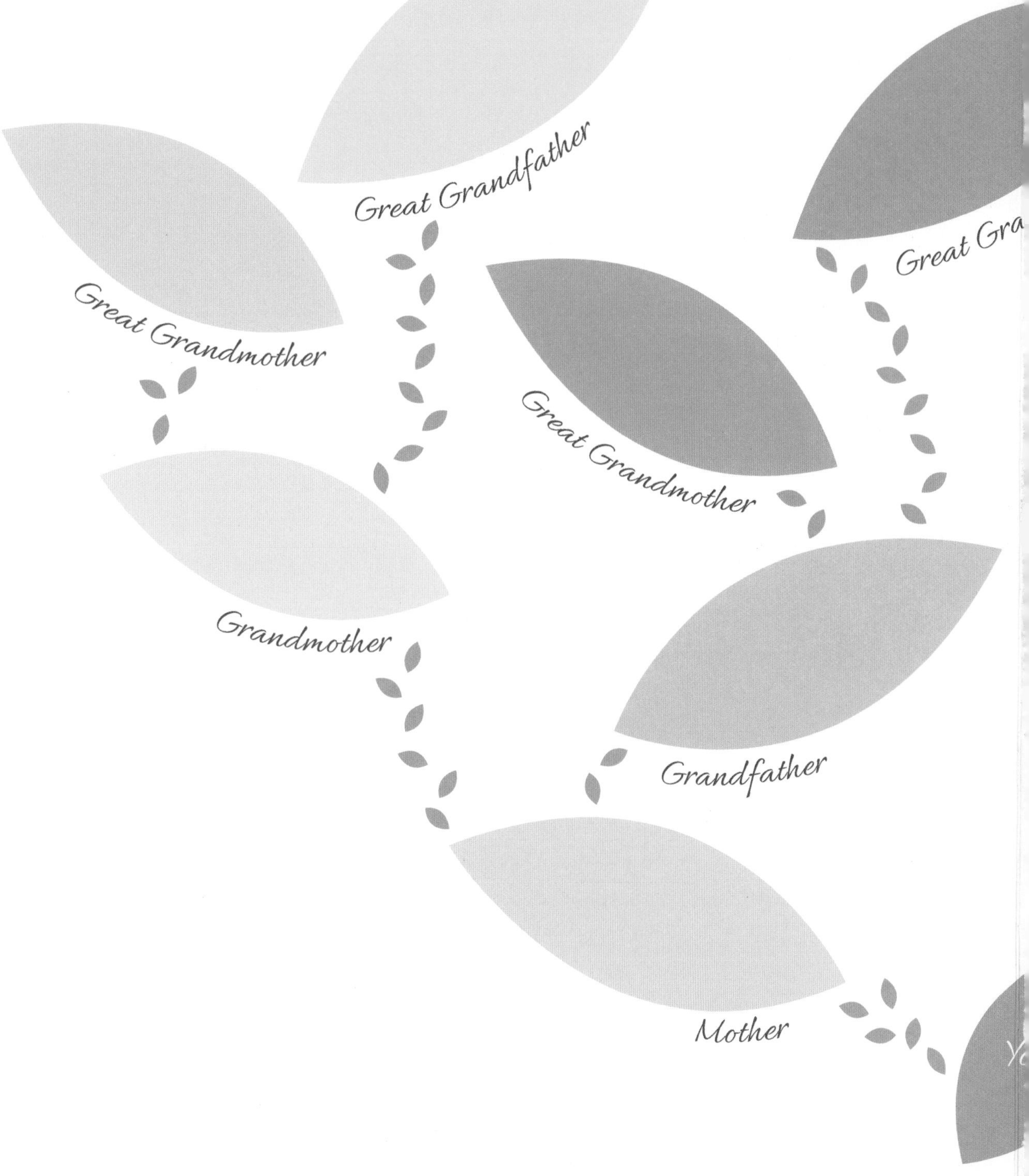

Great Grandfather

Great Grandmother

Great Gra

Great Grandmother

Grandmother

Grandfather

Mother

Yo

Summer Fun

School's out! As a child, this is what I did for fun during the summer _____

_____

_____

This is the biggest difference between summertime for kids today compared

to my childhood _____

_____

_____

I went to this camp as a child _____

_____

_____

It was located in _____

I attended this camp for _____ years.

Here is a camp story I shared with my children _____

_____

_____

_____

_____

Family Reconnections

My family comes together every _____ for a reunion.

It is traditionally held _____

These are the family members who usually attend _____

_____

_____

_____

The person who travels farthest to attend is _____

_____

who comes all the way from _____

_____

I most look forward to this part of the reunion _____

_____

_____

_____

This is a story about my family that never gets old _____

_____

_____

_____

The most emotional family reunion was _____

_____

_____

Food is a huge part of family reunions. Here is a description of a typical spread _____

_____

_____

_____

_____

The treat I most look forward to is _____

_____

_____

It's made by _____

A traditional game, activity, or competition that we have at family reunions is _____

_____

_____

_____

The winner of this event usually is _____

_____

_____

Place photo here

Place photo here

Place photo here

Place photo here

Place photo here

Place photo here

Happy Birthday to You!

My family celebrates birthdays with this special tradition _____

_____

_____

When I was a child, this is what birthday parties were like _____

_____

_____

My children's or grandchildren's parties are different because _____

_____

_____

One particular birthday celebration that stands out in my memory is _____

_____

_____

My most memorable birthday gift as a child was _____

_____

_____

This person usually bakes the birthday cakes for our parties _____

_____

_____

Place photo here

This is a special birthday cake recipe that we use in our family _____

_____

_____

_____

_____

_____

_____

_____

_____

Weekly Wonders

These were some weekly family traditions my family had when I was growing up

_____

_____

_____

This is my fondest memory of this event _____

_____

_____

Today, I share this tradition with _____

_____

_____

Place photo here

Place photo here

Place photo here

Place photo here

Place photo here

Place photo here

Place photo here

Place photo here

 # Spiritual Richness

I am this religion _____

It is / is not the same religion I grew up with.

This is how important religion was in my childhood home _____

_____

This is how important religion is in my home _____

_____

I did / did not raise my children with this religion.

When there is marriage in our family, these religious traditions are honored _____

_____

_____

When a baby is born in my family, these religious ceremonies are performed _____

_____

_____

Here is a story connected to this event _____

_____

_____

_____

_____

And the Title Goes To...

According to family reputation, tradition, and, of course,
legendary folklore, assign a family member's name to
each of the following titles. Remember...this is all good fun!!

Advice columnist in waiting _____

Animal fan _____

Artist _____

Blue-ribbon baker _____

Cuddle expert _____

Diva _____

Drama king or queen _____

Favorite photographer _____

First-place athlete _____

Friend to all _____

Gold-medal cook _____

Green thumb _____

Honorary beauty pageant winner _____

Inventive genius _____

Knee-slappin' comic _____

Legendary storyteller _____

Most creative mind _____

Penny-pincher _____

Political activist _____

Prankster _____

Problem solver _____

White-glove housekeeper _____

Wild child (age is irrelevant) _____

Place photo here

Place photo here

Place photo here

Place photo here

Place photo here

Place photo here

Place photo here

Place photo here

Tall Tales, Big Laughs

This is my favorite family story _____

_____

_____

_____

_____

_____

_____

_____

_____

_____

_____

_____

_____

_____

_____

Tall Tales, Big Laughs

This is a story that my children enjoy repeating... much to my chagrin _____

_____

_____

_____

_____

_____

_____

_____

_____

_____

_____

_____

_____

_____

Tall Tales, Big Laughs

This is a story that my children enjoy repeating... much to my chagrin _____

_____

_____

_____

_____

_____

_____

_____

_____

_____

_____

_____

_____

_____

_____

_____

Tall Tales, Big Laughs

This is a story that my children enjoy repeating... much to my chagrin _____

_____

_____

_____

_____

_____

_____

_____

_____

_____

_____

_____

_____

_____

9 to 5
and
Beyond

It's a Family Affair

Here is a description of the family-owned business that adult children in my family

naturally went into _____

_____

_____

I did / did not go into the business.

My children will / will not go into this family business.

This is how my children feel about their professional heritage _____

_____

_____

Here are a few details about the history of this family business—how it began and how

it changed over the years _____

_____

_____

This is what my father did for a living _____

_____

Here is how I felt about his career _____

_____

_____

This is how my father dressed to go to work each morning _____

_____

_____

_____

My father gave me this advice about selecting a career _____

_____

_____

_____

Place photo here

My mother did / did not have a career outside of the home.

Here is a description of her work _____

_____

_____

_____

These were the career choices that were available to women when I was growing up

_____

_____

_____

Place photo here

Place photo here

These were the career choices that were available to women when I was a young adult

_____

_____

This is a woman in my family history who bucked tradition and went on to achieve

great things _____

_____

_____

Here is a description of what she did _____

_____

_____

She faced these roadblocks while pursuing her career _____

_____

_____

Here is the advice my mother gave me on the subject of choosing a career _____

_____

_____

_____

 # Pocket Change

My first after-school job was _____

_____ when I was _____ years old.

A typical job for people my age was _____

_____

_____

_____

_____

My pay was _____

This was / was not a good rate at the time.

I used my paycheck for _____

_____

_____

_____

Other jobs I had were _____

_____

_____

_____

The Corporate Ladder

My first career-related position was _____

_____

_____

I began my career when _____

_____

_____

Here is a description of my career path _____

_____

_____

_____

When I first started working, this is what corporate life was like _____

_____

_____

_____

Here is how things have changed in the corporate world since my first job _____

_____

_____

_____

Place photo here

Place photo here

Place photo here

Place photo here

Place photo here

Place photo here

Military Service

These people in our family pursued a military career _____

_____

_____

Here is a description of their military service _____

_____

_____

_____

This is the advice I would give my child or grandchild about joining the military

_____

_____

_____

When I was a young adult, this was the country's attitude toward the military system

_____

_____

_____

Here is how attitudes have changed _____

_____

_____

Place photo here

Place photo here

Place photo here

Place photo here

Our Medical History

Heredity is linked to many diseases and conditions. Today, medical technology can often prevent these conditions from developing—especially if your family has a medical tree.

Note any family members who had the following diseases or conditions. Include significant dates, such as approximate date of diagnosis and how old the person was when diagnosed. Also include any known medical reason for the disease or condition.

Allergies, including asthma _____

_____

Alzheimer's disease _____

_____

Cancer (specify type) _____

_____

Cystic fibrosis _____

_____

Depression, anxiety, or other psychiatric illness _____

_____

Diabetes _____

_____

Eye diseases _____

_____

Hearing loss _____

_____

Heart diseases _____

_____

High blood pressure _____

_____

Huntington's disease _____

_____

Learning or mental disabilities _____

_____

Parkinson's disease _____

_____

Polycystic kidney disease (PKD) _____

_____

Reproductive conditions _____

_____

Sickle cell anemia _____

_____

Other _____

Special

Notes

This is one piece of advice I would like to pass on to future generations _____

_____

_____

_____

_____

_____

_____

_____

_____

_____

_____

_____

_____

_____

This is something I would like to say to my children _____

_____

_____

_____

_____

_____

_____

_____

_____

_____

_____

_____

_____

_____

_____

This is something I would like to say to my grandchildren _____

_____

_____

_____

_____

_____

_____

_____

_____

_____

_____

_____

_____

_____

_____

_____

_____

_____

This is something I would like to say to my great grandchildren _____

_____

_____

_____

_____

_____

_____

_____

_____

_____

_____

_____

_____

_____

_____

Place photo here

Place photo here

Place photo here

Place photo here

Place photo here

Place photo here